INHALT/CONTENT

Deutsch — 1

1996 — 1
1997 — 5
1998 — 9
1999 — 21

English — 37

1996 — 37
1997 — 51
1998 — 65
1999 — 81

DEUTSCH
1996

Vergessene Träume.

Verlorene Lichter,

in dem See es Spiels.

Insgeheim hoffen auf den Moment

einer spielerischen Glückseligkeit.

Einmal wieder sehen können.

Leichtigkeit bei der Sicht der Sandbank.

Lösen von den Ketten der Vernunft.

Liebe – um einmal die Unendlichkeit zu spüren.

Lust – Freude auf der Spitze des erklommenen Bergs.

Eine Windböe treibt das Boot auf das offene Meer.

Einmal wieder die Weite erblicken.

Ist das Sein so kompliziert?

Immer noch das Lied der Sehnsucht?!

Christen – eine traurige Zukunft!?

Chrysantheme – mit wem blüht sie zusammen?

Heimatlich, doch der Blick schweift in die Ferne.

Hast Du das Licht gesehen?

Transzendenz – ein Spiel oder Glückseligkeit?

Trennt der Weg die Weiden?

Eine Bitte.

Eine Frage.

Eine Antwort?

∞

Was fühlst Du, wenn Deine Hand die Wangen Deines Gegenübers berührt,

wenn Deine Augen über die Deines Gegenübers streifen,

wenn Deine Zunge Bote Deines Herzens wird?

Wer ist Dein Gegenüber?

Wer bewacht Deine Träume,

wenn deren Inhalt Dich nervös macht?

Wer spricht zu Dir,

wenn Du Dich nicht mehr halten kannst,

weil das Verständnis die Schale bricht?

Vom Berg schweifen Deine Augen ins Tal.

Steigt die Sehnsucht wieder auf?

Klamm halten sich die Finger am Stein fest.

War der Stein schon immer da, bestimmt die Größe die Sicht?

Was macht der Stein neben dem Fels,

wenn der Fels ihn nicht sieht?

Welcher Berg steht im Vergleich zu dem,

was ich erschaffe und nicht habe?

Wenn der Kopf vom Himmel fällt,

bringt das Saugen neues Leben?

Einzelne Momente des Höhepunkts,

wie schmerzen die Momente der Enthaltsamkeit?

An wen glaubst Du, wenn Du um Dich schaust?

Wann nimmst Du, weil es dich begehrt?

Wann gibst Du, weil Du möchtest?

Wann wird Risiko ein Teil Deiner selbst?

Wenn die Gesellschaft Freuden zerstört, wofür entscheidest Du Dich?

∞

Ich stelle mir vor, ich gehe;

vielleicht fange ich auch an zu laufen.

An welcher Stelle stehe ich denn jetzt?

Meine Gedanken fliegen, doch sind Worte mühselig.

Augen

Ich sitze auf meiner Schaukel und schwinge hin und her.

War es das jetzt oder kommt vielleicht noch mehr?

Der Kopf ist ein Reich, Gedanken fließen.

An dem Fluss steht ein Weidezaun, selber aufgestellt; darf ich genießen?

Wenn ich rede, sprengen die Welten;

wenn nicht, platzt die Blase.

Während wir für den Winter werben, sendet der Sommer seine Signale.

Und doch stehe ich am Zaun, mein Blick sucht am Horizont.

Wer besitzt die Gaben, das Geschick?

Tiere im Verständnis meiner Seele, wo sind die Nischen für die Deckung?

Es sind Träume, die leben in dieser Welt;

das Meer, man ist auf sich allein gestellt.

Wenn ich wählen muss, so stehe ich auf der Kuppe,

der Wind wird entscheiden, der Nebel ist fort.

Wenn das Leben der Träume in den Augen strahlt,

spiegelt das Bild von Himmel und Sonne

Harmonie

im Herzen wider.

Helden?

∞

DEUTSCH
1997

Ich spreche vom Leben.
Ich spreche vom Geben.
Ich spreche von Freude.
Ich spreche von Glück.

Ich male Bilder.
Ich male Träume.
Ich male Sehnsucht.
Ich male Tränen.

Ich erzähle Geschichten.
Ich erzähle Zukunft.
Ich erzähle Wege.
Ich erzähle Trauer.

Du hörst vom Leben,
wonach willst Du streben?

Wo verliert sich die Sonne im Meer?
Wo verliert sich die Weite in der Ferne?
Wo verliert sich der Sinn in der Illusion?

Vielleicht kommt mit dem Leben die Treue.
Vielleicht kommt mit dem Licht die Höhe.
Vielleicht kommt mit dem Weg das Ziel.

Woran glaubst Du, wenn Du nach oben schaust?
Woran glaubst Du , wenn die Wand vor Dir ist?
Woran glaubst Du, wenn Du auf dem Loch stehst?

Später war es, dass es steht.
Später wird es, dass es bleibt.
Später ist es, dass es geht.

Wie läuft man, wenn man steht?
Wie träumt man, wenn man spricht?
Wie sieht man, wenn man sieht?

Wann wird das Dorf zur Stadt?
Wann wird der Bach zum Fluss?
Wann wird der Versuch zum Glück?

Vielleicht wird der Hügel zum Berg.
Vielleicht wird das Boot zum Schiff.
Vielleicht wird das Mädchen zur Frau.

Wozu glaubst Du, wenn Du weißt?
Wozu weißt Du, wenn Du verstehst?
Wozu verstehst Du, wenn Du siehst?

Darum sei es, wie es ist.
Darum ist es, wie es sein soll.
Darum soll es sein, wie das Sein ist.

Lass das Leben leben,
solange das Leben dem Leben das Leben
schenken kann!

∞

DEUTSCH
1998

Wieviel Jahre? Wieviel Tage?

Sprich zu mir und Du wirst sehen.
Geh dahin und komme wieder.
Setz Dich hin und treibe fort.

Wieviel Zahlen? Wieviel Fragen?

Erkenne es und es erscheint.
Laufe morgen und Du stehst gestern.
Liebe jetzt und träume ewig.

Wieviel Sorgen? Wieviel Nöte?

Denke nach und es erreicht Dich.
Strebe hier und es fließt da.
Frag wofür und es ergibt sich.

Eine schöne neue Welt

∞

Friedlich ist die Welt.

Unbekannt das Sein.

Aufgaben gestellt.

Frei sein ist Dein.

Lass Freiheit uns erleben.

Lass der Treue alles geben.

Lass das Netz für ewig weben.

Es kommt und es geht.

Und es bleibt, wo es steht.

Glück

Träume

Trauer

Geben

Auf das Leben

∞

Lass sie wachsen, die Blumen,

    denn sie werden blühen.

Lass sie träumen, die Menschen,

    denn sie werden sterben.

Lass sie laufen, die Tiere,

    denn sie werden kommen.

Ist es wirklich so, dass

    Kranke sehen können?

Ist es wahr, dass

    Träume unerreichbar bleiben?

Ist es wahrscheinlich, dass

    wir im Angesicht der Idee stehen bleiben?

Endlichkeit der Kranken?

Endlichkeit der Träume?

Endlichkeit der Idee?

    Brauchen wir Beweise, die

        den Himmel zur Erde bringen?

    Brauchen wir die Phantasie, die

        die Erde zum Himmel trägt?

    Brauchen wir die Erde und den Himmel, die

        den Anfang und das Ende bezeichnen?

    Ergeben wir uns der Furcht,

        wenn wir am falschen Ende stehen?

    Ergeben wir uns dem Ganzen,

        wenn wir nur Teile wahrnehmen?

    Ergeben wir uns der Fülle,

        wenn die Leere bereits eintrifft?

''

Lass uns in die Berge ziehen,

     wenn wir uns der Erde nahen.

Lass uns die Blüten erforschen,

     wenn wir uns der Wurzel nahen.

Lass uns mit den Vögeln sprechen,

     wenn wir uns dem Tier am Boden nahen.

Aber warum sollen wir zweifeln,

     wenn das Verständnis ausbleibt?

Aber warum sollen wir begreifen,

     wenn das Ergebnis unseren Erwartungen widerspricht?

Aber warum sollen wir aufstehen,

     wenn der Sitzplatz der gleichen Sichtweise entspricht?

Schwelgen wir in Träumen,

     weil wir uns der Wirklichkeit entziehen wollen?

Schwelgen wir im Daseinschaos,

     weil wir uns anders nicht entwickeln können?

Schwelgen wir in einer subrealen Welt,

     weil sonst die Erträglichkeit sinkt?

Schade, sagen viele,

     weil es nicht noch schöner sein kann.

Schade, glauben viele,

     weil das Bewusstsein nicht größer sein kann.

Schade, sage ich,

     weil ich nicht glaube.

Schuld hat, wer das Licht in den Schatten stellt.

Schuld hat, wer im Wald die Bäume sucht.

Schuld hat, wer in den Träumen die Wahrheit sieht.

Ist es so, dass

     der Anzug des Einzelnen für die Gesamtheit spricht?

Ist es so, dass

     die Uhr weiterläuft, auch wenn der Einzelne stehen bleibt?

Ist es so, dass

     das Zittern des Einzelnen nicht der Kälte der Breite vorangeht?

Eventuell schweben wir auf den Wipfeln der Bäume
ohne die Angst, herunterzufallen.
Eventuell träumen wir am Tag,
weil die Nacht reserviert bleibt.
Eventuell jagen wir die großen Tiere,
weil wir bei den Kleinen uns selber sehen.

Nach uns,
wird die Welt in die Unendlichkeit schweifen?
Nach uns,
wird die Welt unbemerkt vom Rest vorbeiziehen?
Nach uns,
wird die Welt den Weg zurückverfolgen?
In der neuen Welt wird alles wieder besser.
In der neuen Welt wachsen wir wieder voller Freude auf.
In der neuen Welt entsteht wieder ein Gefüge,
das niemand sieht, jeder braucht und keiner zulässt.
Christus kam –
war damals die Hoffnung noch gegeben?
Christus ist gegenwärtig –
in Wirklichkeit oder muss der Glaube reichen?
Christus wird nicht sein –
ist es Blasphemie oder nur die Frage nach dem Sinn?
Hände greifen nach mir –
sinke ich im Wasser auf den Grund?
Hände greifen nach mir –
liege ich auf dem Gras in der Wiese?
Hände greifen nach mir –
gleite ich durch die Luft in den Himmel?
Tasten wir uns nach vorn –
bleibt es wirklich immer so?
Tasten wir uns nach vorn –
gibt uns das vertraute Gefühl auch Sicherheit?
Tasten wir uns nach vorn –
schenkt sie uns auch Ewigkeit?

Nimm mich mit auf dem
>Weg des Daseins der Treue.
Nimm mich mit auf dem
>Weg des Glaubens an ihre Unendlichkeit.
Nimm mich mit auf dem
>Weg der Mittel der Wahrheit.
Und immer wieder versuchen wir es.
Und immer wieder glauben wir daran.
Und immer wieder werden wir enttäuscht.
>Richten wir uns nach ihr oder
>>versuchen wir zu entkommen?
>Richten wir uns nach dem Gegenteil –
>>werden wir das Grauen fassen können?
>Richten wir uns nach unseren Vorstellungen –
>>werden wir ewig träumen?

Eilig gehen wir weiter und
>fassen unser Schicksal nicht.
Eilig versuchen wir es noch mal und
>Frustration umgibt uns.
Eilig finden wir Gründe, die
>uns von der Leere des Inneren ablenken.
Ist die Phantasie
>zur Wirklichkeit geworden?
Ist die Wahrheit
>bereits ins Offene getreten?
Ist der Traum
>schon zu Ende?
Nicht ich, sondern
>die Glaubenden der Welt haben Schuld.
Nicht der Vorgang, sondern
>das Ausmaß sollte verschieden sein.
Nicht die Kraft der Freude, sondern
>die Bekenntnis der Tat hat es ausgemacht.

Teilen wir das Schicksal oder ist
    die Teilhabe das Schicksal?
Teilen wir die Vorwürfe oder ist
    der Vorwurf ein Teil von uns?
Teilen wir die Ewigkeit der Träume oder ist
    ein Teil der Ewigkeit ein Traum von uns?
Respektieren wir die Wahl –
    ist sie das Einzige, was uns bleibt?
Respektieren wir den Lauf der Geschichte –
    wo ist der Grund, etwas zu verändern?
Respektieren wir die Endgültigkeit –
    ist das Gegenteil der Fall?
Abgegeben war die Stimme –
    bewirkte sie mehr als das Symbol?
Abgegeben war das Blut –
    bewirkte es mehr als das Symbol?
Abgegeben war die Wärme –
    bewirkte sie mehr als das Symbol?
Umgehen wir den Berg,
    denn er könnte zu gewaltig sein.
Umgehen wir den Fluss,
    denn er könnte zu reißend sein.
Umgehen wir das Feuer,
    denn es könnte zu heiß werden.
Menschen sind krank –
    sind sie unglücklich?
Menschen sterben –
    sind sie glücklich?
Menschen leben –
    sind sie glücklicher?

Selbst sein eigener Herr zu sein –

        können wir das überhaupt?

Selbst sein eigenes Ich kennen –

        sollen wir das überhaupt?

Selbst seine wahren Gefühle leben –

        dürfen wir das überhaupt?

Ewige Verbundenheit –

        kann das alles sein?

Ewige Verbundenheit –

        gibt es etwas schöneres?

Ewige Verbundenheit –

        wird es so bleiben?

Immer wieder neue Hoffnung schöpfen –

        wahrhaftig.

Immer wieder neu Vertrauen bilden –

        wahrhaftig.

Immer wieder neue Freude schenken –

        wahrhaftig.

Niemals völlig hingeben und

        ruhig wird das Leben bleiben.

Niemals das Gefühl verspüren und

        geordnet wird das Leben bleiben.

Niemals die Welt in anderem Licht sehen und

        beständig wird das Leben bleiben.

!!!

Es wird.

Wird es?

∞

Für Dich.
Nur.

Hier, immer, jetzt, alles.
Für Dich, dennoch, schon, ja.
Wieder, schön, gleich, trotzdem.
Lass, gib, zieh, Treue.

Hier bin ich, ich freue mich.
Immer bist Du bei mir, Gedanken fließen.
Jetzt wirst Du mein, Du fühlst es.
Alles möchte ich Dir geben, Liebe ist.

Für Dich schreibe ich Geschichte, der Fluss im Sein.
Dennoch erscheinst Du im Schein, die Bewunderung naht.
Schon beginne ich zu träumen, ein jedes seinen Weg.
Ja, Du siehst mich, der Aufmerksamkeit soll es.

Wieder gleichst Du dem Wind, Lüfte erheben mich.
Schön, dass ich die Haut spüren darf, die Weichheit Deiner.
Gleich ergehe ich der Vision, das ewige Eins.
Trotzdem darf der Zweifel nicht kommen, Schicksal, so ist es.

Lass das Zusammensein die Zeit bestimmen, nur so.
Gib dem Zauber Zeit zum Ziehen, glaube ja.
Zieh nicht vor, zurückzugehen, es kommt.
Treue der Tiefe, der Kern ist alles; Sein darf nicht anders sein.

Nicht nur für alles.
Du.

∞

DEUTSCH
1999

Ich sagte, hör auf.
Glaubst Du mir nicht?
Träumer, Helden,
– Versager –

Weiche dem Glück, es steht.
Weiche dem Gang, er verläuft sich.
Weiche dem Berg, er bleibt.
Auch Du solltest nicht fragen.
Auch Du solltest nicht geradeaus gehen.
Auch Du solltest nicht treiben.
Ruf mich an , ich sollte da sein.
Ruf es an, es sollte antworten.
Ruf ihn an, er sollte Dich erwarten.
Unter uns, haben viele gesagt.
Unter uns, da trennten sich die Wege.
Unter uns, da verlief sich die Spur.
Mich hast Du nicht gesehen.
Mich wirst Du nicht halten.
Mich wirst Du nicht vermissen.

Kein Geld der Welt – haben viele gesagt.
Kein Glück auf Erden – bist Du sicher?
Kein Traum, der erfüllt – ist es Schicksal?
Ohne alles, das wollten viele.
Ohne mich, glaubst Du auch daran?
Ohne Visionen –Träumer, wenn nicht.
Mit mir – schweift die Seele.
Mit den gegebenen Gaben –gibt es das?
Mit allen Helden – wie entsteht die Welt?
Mach es, dass es gut wird.
Mach es, dass es wieder beginnt.
Mach es, dass sie wieder aufleben.

Sicher waren viele – bevor sie den Aufstieg begannen.

Sicher waren alle, als sie das Licht erblickten.

Sicher warst Du, als Du mein sagtest.

Träume weiter – es lohnt sich.

Trau Dich nicht – warum weiß keiner.

Tausend und eine Nacht – warum?

Denn alles ist gut; ist es das?

Denn die Hoffnung lebt, jawohl.

Denn alle wollten dabei sein, sicher, sicher.

Umständlich ist nur die Sperre.

Unverständlich ist nur die Ansicht.

Unverzüglich ist nur das nicht Geschehene.

Nicht allein willst Du sein.

Nicht vorhanden, träumst Du immer noch?

Nicht, weil Du es bist – Du bist es nicht.

In Dir schwelgt das Licht.

In mir leuchtet die Leere.

In dem Weg werden wir geblendet

– soll ich oder soll ich nicht lachen?

Christine war nicht der Name – warum?

Chamäleon – wer traut Dir noch?

Chloroform – ohne würde es nicht nur.

Heimat – verbirgst Du Dein wahres Ich?

Heimat – fasse zusammen Dein Bleiben.

Heimat – bleibst oder kommst Du wieder?

Tumulte – worum geht die Erregung?

Tust Du es wirklich – nicht?

Traust Du mir eher nicht – doch?

???

Schon wieder

∞

Frag mich mehr,
ich weiß zuviel.
Wer sagt, das Sein sei
soviel – so sei es.

Warum steht,
was niemals weitergeht,
doch für die Zeit
ist es, dass es
nicht nur so bleibt?!

Hörst Du mich?
Ich wiederhole mich nicht gerne.

Gehe von Abstand aus;
hilft er Dir wirklich?
Lächeln hilft Dir weiter,
sagen alle, sage ich.

Glaube ich daran?
Nicht wirklich.

Schadet der Versuch dessen?
Nicht wirklich.

Schadet der Versuch an sich?
Nicht wirklich.

Glaube daran, vielleicht hilft Dir das weiter;
Mir auch;
na ja, nicht entschieden.

Nachdem es kam,
wird es sein,
werden wir es sehen.

Vielleicht.
Glücklich ist der,
der nicht weiß,
dass es nicht gibt,
was sein sollte
und niemals sein wird.

Hilfe brauchen die,
die wissen, was es nicht gibt,
aber dem Glauben verfallen,
dass das Wissen trotzdem vorhanden ist.

Verzweifelt sind die,
die wissen, was es nicht gibt,
und die Endlosigkeit erkennen.

Die anderen sind die,
die nicht darauf gekommen sind.

Sei es, wie es ist.
So sei es, wie es ist.
So wird es sein, wie es ist.

Für alle, die nicht wissen.
Für alle, die glauben zu wissen.
Für alle, die wissen,
und vor allem für die anderen.

Ich denke,
dass es so sein könnte;
nein, nicht wirklich.
Oder doch?

So wird es sein.

∞

Herzschmerz,
träume jetzt und hier.
Wonach es auch klingt, doch es ist, es ist wahr.

Ich träume und lebe.
Den Traum zu leben,
darf kein Traum bleiben.
Tränen fließen, ich denke,
mein Herz ist rein,
doch was passiert – ich bin allein.
Allein nicht wirklich,
denn Du bist mein.
Ich stehe auf und möchte singen,
das Glück schwingt mit mir.
Gesang – nein, nicht aus meinem Munde,
darum schreibe ich
für Dich
– für immer –
möchte ich sein
mit dir.

In dem Wissen, dass du dies verstehst
bin ich, bin ich,
einfach glücklich.

Sei frei, werde sein.
Die Flügel schwingen
mit meiner Seele,
das ist die Deine,
das ist die Meine
und
eins sind wir.

Das Melodrama der Ewigkeit,
– unbeschreiblich –
der Schmerz, der
Dich übermannt,
wenn die Zärtlichkeit zu sein hat.
Verlust untragbar; ich weiß,
er wird nicht sein,
denn Du bist mein
und
eins sind wir.

Träume sind keine Illusion,
Wirklichkeit macht sie wahr.
Unsere Wirklichkeit.
Zufriedenheit.
Lass andere suchen,
wir sind weiter,
bereits;
froh können wir sein.
Freude umgibt uns,
Schmerzen werden erträglich,
das Wissen hilft uns weiter.
Du umgibst mich
und
eins sind wir.

Ich schweife über Deinen Wolken,
Hüter der Unglaublichkeit.
Lass uns nicht länger warten,
der Verdienst ist unser;
dafür und für alles andere,
für alles, was kommen mag.
Du gibst mich nicht mehr her,
ich will es so
und
eins sind wir.

Tränen erklären Überschwang

an dem emotional

Unfassbaren.

Augen, Deine bedeuten alles.

Fessele mich damit

auf alle Zeit

und

eins sind wir.

Ich höre nicht, gebe nicht auf,

das Schicksal will es;

ich gebe Dich

niemals mehr her

und

eins sind wir.

Es fällt mir schwer,

Gefühle, meine, in Worte zu fassen

– warum ? –

weil sie unendlich sind

und

eins sind wir.

Es war der Moment und er sagt,

alles, einfach alles,

was ich sagen möchte und zu sagen habe.

Ein Umreißen der Gefühle.

Mein Traum ist Wirklichkeit.

Danke

∞

Kaum gesehen und schon weg.
Freude in der Seele.
Erfüllt sind wir,
dennoch überwiegt das Positive.
Denn wir waren da und haben gesehen.

Und das Leben geht weiter.
Und wir stehen woanders.
Und die Sonne wird scheinen.
Und wir werden das Leben genießen,
uns auf den Körper beziehen,
uns auf die Freiheit berufen,
uns für die Zukunft empfehlen.
Und weich und zart, das war schön.
Und hart und fest, nötig war es.
Und leicht und beschwingt, entlastet ist es.
Und schwer und erdrückend, vorbei ist es.
Uns lacht es entgegen.
Uns steht es weinend gegenüber.
Uns ist es vorangegangen.
Und es lächelt und singt.

Ich schreite weiter,
gehe meinen Weg,
die Sterne sind so nah.

Auf die Freiheit, auf das Leben.
Auf die besten,
denn sie werden vernachlässigt,
behindert und verschmäht.

Doch sie sind besser.

∞

Ich war da.
Du nicht.
Keinen Grund – warum auch nicht.

Ich träume in Sehnsucht von dem,
was vergangen sein sollte.
Ich verlasse die Zukunft,
gehe weiter ins Dasein.
Ich lebe die Vorstellung,
zerbrochen – so oder so.

Einst gedachte ich dem Glauben;
glaubte, dass zu tragen die Hoffnung gedeihe;
gediehen war allein das Gezeichnete;
gezeichnet war, dennoch ließ es los;
losgelassen geriet das Bild in Schieflage;
schief gelegen, um so größer der Schritt;
geschritten, gerannt und dennoch vermeidbar;
vermieden, verschmäht, nur zu wahren;
gewahrt, in den Gedanken zu bleiben;
geblieben ist, was begann zu verjähren;
verjährt war, dennoch zu trotzen;
getrotzt, aber allein mag es erschweren;
erschwert zum Sein, jeder zu wachsen;
gewachsen, dennoch das Bild zu verzerren;
verzerrt genügt, das Gehen zu lernen;
gelernt, gemäßigt, frei der Vermutung;
vermutet, dennoch unterstützen wir die Annahme;
angenommen, es wäre so, wir stehen weiter,
weiter, immerzu weiter, der Schrei wird lauter.

∞

Tretet ein, mein Geschenk wird Eures sein.
Kommt, fangt an, sonst wird es traurig sein.
Kümmert Euch, bemüht Euch, es soll so sein.
Nehmt alles mit, es wird nicht mehr von Nöten sein.
Haltet die andere Wange hin, die Realität muss Schmerz wohl sein.

Wir beginnen zu glauben; zu glauben,
dass sich alles wiederholt.
Der Kreislauf schürt die Sinne und einst war es,
dass sich Leben wiederholt.
Vor den Weichen des Weges stehend, wissen wir,
dass sich alles wiederholt.
Dennoch meinen wir, grundsätzlich können wir,
das Neue ist allgegenwärtig.
Wir sind ja an der Spitze, überhaupt die Spitze,
es gibt nur uns.
Wir entsprechen dem, was durchdachte der,
dem es entspricht, zu denken.
Immer wieder und vielleicht auch nicht.

Der Zweifel trägt die Sinne.
Die Vernunft als Versuch zu bändigen.
Die Tugend umschreibt den Irrglauben.
Der Schein lässt den Spiegel zeichnen.
Der Traum in dem Versuch zu bündeln.
Die Illusion in dem Versuch es zu ertragen.
Die Realität als Annahme der Beschreibung.
Die Entschuldigung nur um zu wahren.
Der Glaube lässt uns weiter schreiten.

Wann werden wir uns treu sein?

∞

Ich sah sie. Sie schrieb.
Wir gingen weiter und wir standen.
Glänzen in den Augen, der Trübe zunichte.

Sie stand am Wasser, den Strom hinauf.
Sie blickte auf den Turm, die Glocken läuteten.
Sie erschien im Traum, den Weg weisend.
Ich stand am Wasser und sah das Boot.
Ich blickte auf den Turm und sah die Spitze.
Ich erschien im Traum und sah mein Herz.

Vergänglich zu denken, vorsehend war es.
Bereitend zu gehen, schmal war es.
Gleichzeitig zu brauchen, genießend war es.
Und wir blieben da und lachten.
Und wir vollendeten zusammen und gaben.
Und wir schieden wieder und erfreuten.

Interessant, der Schein zu sein.
Informell zu trauen – die Öffnung.
Innerlich hingeben der Muße – Stärke.
    Charismatisch – das Auftreten erleuchtet.
    Christus war da – leider nicht mitgelaufen.
    Cummulus – auch hier vielleicht zuviel.
Hinterblieben – allein kann Form sein.
Herausgefordert – allein kann Form sein.
Hinunterschauen – allein kann Form sein.

Größe war die Gabe – es lohnt sich wofür?
Gegeben steht geschrieben – es verweigert wenig?
Gloria in Vernunft – es mutet an?
    Lachen getragen und wieder erreichte sie.
    Lieblich in Taten und gemäßigt vollendet.
    Lust an sich in Grenzen und sie trotzte.

Aufschrei kommt – sollen wir in Bahnen lenken?
Angebot erzielt – streichen wir nach und nach?
Austausch gewährt – war die Lösung so weit entfernt?
    Unternommen hat sie alles, doch es war wieder bewusst.
    Unterfangen eingeläutet, doch sie als Strebsame griff höher.
    Umgebung, in welcher sie war, doch das Umfeld sprach dafür.
Bleibe doch hier; sie sprach und ging.
Belass es doch; sie fand es und trug.
Billige doch; sie erforschte und blieb.
    Einmal waren wir da – beschenkt und bereichert.
    Einst kamen wir wieder – beschenkt und bereichert.
    Einst liebten wir einmal – beschenkt und bereichert.

Nur weil sie es aussprach – ich suchte weiter.
Nur weil sie es tat – ich glaubte nicht.
Nur weil sie sich die Illusion versprach – ich träumte.
    Umso aller in des Widerspruchs vorangeschritten.
    Umso mehr hing das Herz, unser Wort des Fadens Last.
    Unweigerlich führte die Versuchung des Letzten hinaus.
Reibend an Scheiben, vollführt auf der Insel.
Rundherum am Einzelnen, getrieben des Wassers Bote.
Revanchierend an Geleit, nur geführt des Kontrasts.

Einzigartig an Bleibe getroffen, trotzdem ging sie.
Einzig an genauster Stelle geschnitten, trotzdem hielt sie.
Einzigartig an Blicken geheftet, trotzdem verschloss sie.
    Wieder einmal des Weges Beginn suchend gefunden.
    Wieder einmal des Glaubens Ende beraubend gesehen.
    Wieder einmal des Fortschritts Freiheit zaudernd gestanden.
Ich für mich nicht wirklich trauernd – doch Deiner.
Ich für Dich nicht zeitlich bindend – doch meiner.
Ich für Euch nicht peinlich öffnend – doch ihrer.
    Glaube an die Bestimmung – umgeben von beiden.
    Glaube an die Wirklichkeit – umgeben von beiden.
    Glaube an die Unschätzbarkeit – umgeben von beiden.

Die Form der Fassung verblieb als Ganzes.
Und wenn ich sehe, erblicke ich wieder.
Grenzenlos im Sein, es wird bleiben.

Die Form besticht, unveränderlich trotz allem
Die Fassung geformt, Normen nicht verweilt.
Verblieben ist alles, doch teilweise angenommen.
Das Ganze steht sicher, unbefestigt ist gefestigt.
Und wenn es wieder bevorsteht, gestützt ist es.
Ich sehe nicht nur alles, sondern das Ganze als Eins.
Erblickt in Freude vermählt; zu frieren ist falsch.
Ich, wieder in Hoffnung, schmeichle der Sinnessicht.
Grenzenlos waren die Mauern, jenes danach auch.

Im Sein zu erquicken, lebendig ist dieser Trumpf.
Es wird, wie das Werden als geworden nur zu werden wird.
Geblieben ist der Glanz des Aufbaus aus Trümmern.

Im Glauben
wir schwroren.

Geschworen
im Glauben
für jenes, welches
für Glauben zu schwören ist.

Ewig.

∞

Lass mich zum Ende statt Deiner gehen.

Werte geschönt, der Glauben sich gefreut.

Immer noch, nicht wirklich bleib´ ich stehen.

Das Kind den Brunnen gesehen und bereut,

Jenes gebar und den Weg trug es weiter;

Die Schönheit aller im Gegensatz verweilt.

Und wieder rief der Wind dem Baum die Neider,

Vom Schicksal verführt und davon geeilt.

Unbefangen des Ufers und die Blume blüht;

Weiter geschritten in Vorfreude treu geblieben.

Der Strahlen gezähmt, auch was sich rührt,

Lass den Weg das Ziel an sich schmiegen.

Und wenn allein den Weg ich schreite,

Dann nur gemeinsam suchen wir die Weite.

∞

ENGLISH
1996

11/96 EI

Priorities

A hundred years from now it will not matter what your bank account was, the sort of house you lived in, or the kind of car you drove ...

but the world may be different because you were important in the life of a child.

by anonymous

For all the reasons that are one.

The code of making sense

to the ones who care.

Visions

– expressed as dreams –

beyond understanding

picturing moments of fulfillment.

The drive towards happiness.

Love – Joy – Life

Expansion

For all that matters becomes obvious,

the ocean answers with the picture.

Reminiscences bring relief to the staggered mind

when the sequence ends.

Reaching the highest level

by setting priorities.

∞

The morning – Part I
Last night I had dreams.
Dreams that let my body shiver.
Your presence dominated
– flying far.

The ocean's odor was with you
circling the point
where to
we are supposed to go.
The view is clear
yet is the point not visible.
It is too far
since the ocean becomes infinite
for thoughts
so widely spread.

The evening – Part II
The point is only too far
to be caught by the eyes
and the mind
of the wrong one.
If destiny comes into place
the thoughts will center
on the point
and stay.

The night – Part III
Fate can lead
if we
– ourselves –
are ready to see the signs;
recognize the picture.

´Feelings´
´Climax´
´Feelings´
´Struggle´
´Loss´
´Recovery´
´ETL´

May the sky brighten,
may the wind bring fresh air,
may reality be put on hold,
may secrets remain untold,
may deeds excel the words.
Words may vanish;
´destiny´
memories
will center on the point
and stay.
´destiny´

Brainstorming

What do you make,
what do you think of it?

∞

I call for you.
Do you remember the time of spring?
Do you recall what I said about myself,
my dreams, my feelings, my life, my end?
Do you know what I meant by saying
the words which are supposed to bring you the arrows?
Can you reminiscence about events
that took place before they mattered?
Can you feel the hands of the person
moving in godlike ways?
Can you surmise my thoughts by the way
I spread my words?
>Is there an incentive for you to go further???
Is there a chance that you might
consider ways out of standard?
Is there the possibility that you try
to understand perspectives beyond ration?
When I talk about the mountains in my land
do you see the solution to level their tops?
When I take a look over the lakes in my land
do you see the spirits at the bottom?
When I carve the name of life into the woods of my land;
do you see how the spelling is done?
As for what I am, „what am I?", I ask you.
Asking for explanations I pretend not to be the one
questioning your point but looking for you
giving answers about yourself.
What is the call here?

∞

Let my dreams forget how I feel.

May I join the path of joy?

Where can I ask for permission?

Does the admission fee meet my budget?

If I can fly, when I fly, where to do I fly?

Am I missing the details

or do I just pivot on the point

where there is no incentive to step further?!?

I lost track of the path

if there was ever one.

Again and again and again.

When I recover which premise is going to take care

that I bounce off again?

Am I the one to blame for things I think are beyond me?

Where is the entrance to purgatory

for I shiver when I look around!?

– Balance –

on the edge – goals!

Where are the others that understand

for combined forces will point a way:

From the water to the sand, from the sand to the stone.

From the ocean to the island – on the island –

from the beach to the jungle, from the jungle to the mountain.

When I stand at the bottom

of the mountain

I will see

the trail that leads

to the top

only

if I am given a hand

by the one.

The one is the only one

through whom I will be given

clearance to the final stop of the journey

for the stop is where my life will never end.

∞solutions∞

The light flares when I stare intensely

into the right direction.

But the light is not within my sight;

so how do I know?

I am puzzled.

How do I solve the puzzle?

Words are nugatory if the eyes do not comply.

Exonerate me from the creature

that tortures my mind, burns my heart.

Where is the one I can reckon on when the sea loses its composure?

Where is heaven when I can see hell?

Hold on to – even if there is no reason to.

Hang in there – even if you could not care less.

Yearn for the one – your instincts will tell.

You will know what to do.

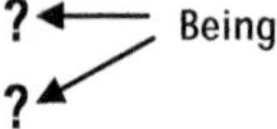

∞

In the morning
Part Alpha

Let me follow the drain.
May I call you innocuous
or does the hidden take chances?
Why is my interest so remote
or is there a pipe that leaks the juice?

Noon
Part Bravo

For its sake – can you let me go?
For what I can have – no answers needed.
For what I might become – what does it offer?
For a status that might not exist – changes needed.
For clandestine affairs – can they be called off?

Afternoon
Part Charly

If there is pride where is the honor?
Succinct words – kept to the essential.
Can I be what I want to be – I may be wrong.
Going a way I despise reading the signs
but missing its story – dismissing its history.

elite

Exacerbate the soul, petrify the heart.
Lavish the mind on the head – is there a need to?
Implacable situations – covered with excrements.
Twist reality – are you worthy?
Enchain the spirit for its vision is without essence.

Evening
Part Foxtrott

Stumble across my lawn.
Send me messages I can read.
Search for a challenge I can master.
Splice my measurements foreseen.
Spike the spot in supposed seekings.

Night
Part Juliet

Are you aware or wary of the angel?

Puzzle my thoughts in the pun of survival.

Who recuperates what has been done?

Take me to get the forgotten.

Where would it be if not there?

Life if lived will prove its life to live by life itself.

When it strikes me do I pursue the bugs on walls?

Take me, wear me, spear me not – just teach.

Will the characters be chosen by the chosen

when the chosen have to choose themselves as chosen?

Late Night
Part Romeo

Call me. I may answer and help with your questions
   for I am gifted
      with talents
         I sometimes wish I had not been given to.

The scorpio may just be an illusion.
   Say life may just be the same,
   say you may just be the one.

Scrape the floor, put on a show

the better the more for life cannot be slow.
   Box me in so I can focus.

Engrave your initials on my soul.

Brand an unlimited drive so infinite
   that it will last forever
      in absolute forms.

Rehearsal
Part Sierra

No forgiving, no repenting, no remunerating.
   Eternity calls for it.

Triumph
Part Victor

Rescue the meaning.

End
Part Zulu

∞

Can my hands make fists?
The punch will follow to the core.
Unchain my hands, let them explore.
The seeking after the unseen, relentless to its point.
When I call you in, tell me the intrinsic pattern.
Do you see the futility in moves uncovered?!
I see the sun – do you see the smile?
At immaculate sight – do you soften?
The burden is heavy if I bear the thoughts alone.
Take me on a trip that leads us
itinerantly through the world – intimacy!
I will share possessions of mine
if you oblige yourself to trying for
salvation.
I know there is a debt – I owe him.
He will demand answers to many questions
regarding scenes that were set in the
past.

For I have to open chapters
– chapters closed and sealed –
that bring back memories
I do not care
to reminiscence about.

But in trust that she will help
there will be no grief
but retrievance
for my soul.

Then for once
sleep
will come.

∞

When it comes to times we all appreciate
we may just call them the
four seasons.

Spring It is when life starts again.

It is when the pleasant takes over.

It is when we blossom along with nature.

Then we may nourish our needs.

Then our smiles may broaden.

Then our lungs may fill with joy.

Then our veins may be injected with hope
just as the leaves turn green.

Summer It is when life becomes simple.

It is when we level the top in entire clearness.

It is when the sky is blue and the sun is at its brightest.

Then we may greet the full picture of joviality.

Then our dreams may burst into achievements.

Then our predilections may become first priority.

Then our lives may dwell without clouds as there are none.

Autumn It is when life changes towards the opposite.

It is when we start looking at what we had.

It is when the energy slowly recedes.

Then we may have to focus on the details again.

Then our body may prepare to slough.

Then our initiative may have to come from the inside.

Then our close ones may have to be bound steadily.

Winter
It is when life is at a close pure range.
It is when your drive needs a fire burning within oneself.
It is when our eyes convey the reflected light shining.
Then we may move cautiously not to destroy the white virgin.
Then our heat may have to pierce through the circumstances.
Then our mind may be wandering to restructure given actions.
Then our feet may find trouble standing steadily.

As for the seasons
our objective may be diverted
for there is more.
Putting the pieces together
we recognize a fully completed circle.
The perfection even if not entirely reached lies within.
The spectrum calls for a massive tribute.
As beauty comes, as beauty stays, as beauty goes
we eventually understand what it is all about.
Permanence of objectives will not guarantee stability
for changes are needed to establish a consistency of balance.
Opposites when challenging fairly
will accommodate a healthy pattern
which will resolve in ultimate leveling.

For fire and water.
For the earth and the sky.
Elements
For men and women.
Priorities by nature.
A circle of balance.

∞

Hey gorgeous, listen up!
Let me tell you a story:
Once upon a lifetime
you kick a stone and wonder,
just wonder why flower seeds come flying,
just wonder why your instincts mislead you,
just wonder why precious moments confuse you.
>Conclusions<
as you might assume clearance.
Preposterous statements inclining temperance.
You look up and think: „Why not me
if I as I am for what I care ask you:
`Do you like to take walks when
the sun still shines but does not blind anymore?`?"
Being confused after wondering,
after concluding thoughts wanting actions
fearing rebuke
you consider what to use to cover your
insecurity.
Finally the decision to move.
Did I miss the stop I had to get out on?
You approach then you contact.
After choosing the right key you unlock
the door
and you start walking.
The `Finish` in sight
you gain speed
and
win.

∞

ENGLISH
1997

Hey, gorgeous, you let me fly again?!
My heart is full of stories,
stories which telling would be worthwhile.
But it cannot be. It is bound by its own.
You asked me why I like flying?
I guess part of it is lightness.
It is that airy feeling that overcomes you.
It is like crossing that line.

That line is the dam

holding my stories

like water.

When I fathom
I come up with something I would like to give.
I just cannot see the slot wherein to fill.
How come I like to sleep?
How come I am glad when I am asleep?
How come the day when waking up
though new and fresh
seems dull and tasteless?
How come although I know what it is
– the drive is missing –
I just cannot help it?

May I cry although my tears are not allowed to dwell?
Why is it that I feel lonely
and it is not getting better?
Why is nobody there to discover my island?
Why is nobody there to answer
the many question I have but cannot answer myself?
Why does anything I start only soothe
my wounds for as long as it is new?
I feel as I relinquish voluntarily
what I really need

but I do not know where to get it.
Give me life or give me death.
Give me dreams or give me answers.
Give me destiny or give me options.
Give me a key or open the vault.
Give me joy or take my hopes.

Set my place or let me vanish.
Show me the light or explain the clouds to me.
Spare me, save me or show me the weapons you will use.

Let me believe in fate or tell me the truth.
Kill the doubts or raise the scale.
I ask questions which are questioned by the questioner.
As the questioner speaks for himself I am questioned.
Answers,
forbidden to be questions
instil doubts beyond removal.

Can it end as it should
or should it end as it will
or will it end as the story tells.

Is the story full of holes?
Are the holes filled with lies
as they lie within their stories?

Stories will be told, someday.

∞

For you my love

Who told us we were believers?
Who said we could join in just like that?
Who asked when we took what we wanted?
Who remembered to look like they expected?
Who drew the circle where we all stand in?
Who said life was fun?

What did they want when they came after us?
What were they looking for when they built the traps?
What did they see when they turned the wrong way?
What did they think when the recognition failed?
What did they feel when they stepped onto the flame?
What did they say life was for?

How did they handle a love incomparable?
How did they take care of the debts unpaid?
How did they go along when love pointed out a way?
How did they pick their choices when love gave a chance?
How did they live with what they wanted so desperately?
How did they say was life to be lived?

Taking up the three essential questions
we conclude for ourselves:

Let us envision the richest of all dreams.
Let us dream the richest of all lives,

rich of love,
rich of joy,
rich of happiness.

Let us concentrate on the focus of life.
Let us focus on the priorities in life.

Symmetry of love

Symmetry of life

Symmetry of giving life with love

Let our minds wander to the richest of visions.
Let us envision the richest of all moments,

rich of love,
rich of clarity,
rich of infinity.

For our love is all we shall ever need.

∞

Poetry in the end,
or does life come first?

Did I tell you joy was an option?
Did I suggest peace was not a goal?
Did the poems break the news?
Or was it just another bubble
waiting for its end to come?
Or was it just another question
remaining in its place unanswered?
Or was it just another cloud
moving west while going east?

Yes I uttered when you asked.
Yes, I stood my ground when they tried me.
Yes, I upheld my vision when she offered the concrete.
Or did I doubt my words?
Or did I just step back not feeling the loss?
Or did I just fear the change moving along with facts?
Use my life, take my body, take my soul.
Use simplicity since they have made me forget the complex.
Use anything you like; I do not care anymore.

Reach me while you can.
Rest when you cannot find me.
Rule over your kingdom, it is yours now.
Ever the optimist?
Ever the primus?
Ever the doubtless?
Ask them, they know everything.
Ask me and I might not know the answer.
Ask yourself who will get you there.
Losing sucks you told me.
Lost you I had when your mind walked away.
Liberated was the heart you had taken.

Lessen the pain was the order given to my senses.
Like the stand of a sandcastle against the flood.
Life was flushed away in seconds.
Yearning after bliss in dreams fulfilled.
You came and begged for another chance.
Yes, I agreed for one more time.

Mess with me and you will lose.
Make me happy and you can only gain.
Mindless games as life is listed.
End as endings only end if lose ends end.
End your game; the only party playing took a break.
Endure your play and you will see it flush.
After sundown I can feel the emptiness.
And scary thoughts overcome me.
Ask me and I might deliver clues.
Never again will I let it happen.
Never again will I open the gate.
Never again will I bear the pain.

Is it love you ask for?
Is it pain you need?
Is it lies you get?
Talk to me and I might help.
Tell me what I need to know.
Take me to your entrance.

???

May life come first
as poetry is sought to be forever.

∞

Hi gorgeous. It is October again.
Are you up to listening?
Besides the few questions that always are present
there are others, maybe new, maybe just slightly defined.
I swore I would take care
of myself, of my life, of my future.
But it seems not to work out.
The princess is flying above as
I am sailing in a nutshell unnoticed.
>Do I care?!?<
Once the question is raised its repetition loses its meaning.
The staggering pain has become an itching particle
below any recognition that bothers.
The tale failure does not leave marks anymore.

Was I chosen not to be judged by people in subjective?
Was I chosen to dismiss the system and stand beside?
Was I chosen to lead the few who exist?
Hi I said and was lost by sight of face.
Height in character is leveled by minds in vastness.
Helpless hopes blankly sustained by incapability.
Asking for answers that allow access.
As honesty is to be sold out.
And commitment is looked upon as distracting.
Tell me what to say and my frequency will not fit.
Tasks given where results are voluntary.
Tales set in stone whose weight is set on feathers.
Thoughts unwanted by the simple.
Thoughts accompanying wishes forever undelivered.
Thoughts occurring any time causing trouble.
Hiring prospects the street has no option for.
Hiring the life out of the origin, whatever it was.
Hiring the conclusion of facts deeming the inevitable.
Enduring the way no one would opt for.
Enduring the stories no one would listen to.
Enduring the end as an end no one would wish for.

Feel like you want and nobody will care.
Follow described pattern but boredom always gets you.
Fancy pictures hanging on rusty hooks.
Undo any tidings and they will still be there.
Utter the great words and there is no one to grasp.
Usher alignments in phrases and the few might not be present.
Cables from one end to the other without connection.
Cuts in places where stitches cannot help.
Curious looks received when the disheveled is spoken.
Kill the doubts and you have lost what is to lose.
Kilos of hearts stuffed in the freezer – no need.
Kill me and the world is lost.

??? – or is it just me?

I probably miss the point again.
...need help?!

If your hand can reach
low enough....

∞

I do not know why I am writing to you.

Maybe I want answers which you cannot give me.
Maybe I want dreams fulfilled wherein you do not participate.
Maybe I want a life I never had but still ask you for.
Maybe I want peace as you only gave me trouble.
Maybe I want a cause for which you did not stand.
Maybe I want the boat which you cannot steer.
Slowly I am drifting apart.
To the North, to the South, to the East, to the West.
As I am moving to all directions
I am still standing.

Maybe it is not what I am but what I want to be.
Maybe it is not the present but just the future.
Maybe it is not the dream but what the illusion gives.
Maybe it is not the strength but just the option.
Maybe it is not the goal but what the way means.
Maybe it is not the what but just the why.
Why do I cry when I lie
in bed helpless
of all the options
I have
but do not care about?

Maybe it is the people's expectations in life
which I look upon as meaningless.
Maybe it is the people's happiness about things
which I look upon as meaningless.
Maybe it is the people's proudest deeds in life
which I look upon as meaningless.
Maybe it is the people's minds as they think
which I recognize as too little.

Maybe it is the people's looks as they appear
which I recognize as too little.
Maybe it is the people's horizon as they glow
which I recognize as too little.

As I do things of interest,
things,
a great number of people deem
interesting
I lose the drive and
bore myself to death.
Again and again and again.

Love me and I loveth thee.
Give me and I giveth thee.
Live me and I liveth thee.

As I lose the style I lose
the last thing I took interest in,
I cared about.
Nothing left.

Is Nothing Something?
Is the loss the gaining?
Is death life?

What do I care?!

∞

Do you remember the times we used to sit and laugh?
Do you remember the times we used to jump and reach the sky?
Do you remember the times we used to fly and not come back?
Do you remember the times we used to call out and achieve?

What do you think the day before Christmas?
What do you think the day after?
What do you think when you guess it has all changed?
What do you think when you wake up and it feels all different?

Sometimes I wonder if the mountain reaches up to its peak.
Sometimes I wonder if the sea makes it down to its depth.
Sometimes I wonder if the sky knows its height.
Sometimes I wonder if the earth feels its soil down under.

What happens when the snow falls in just one direction.
What happens when the man comes just one way.
What happens when the tree points just to the upper.

Do you really recall the scene?
Do you really recall the way?
Do you really recall the option?

Maybe it is bliss for just the moment.
Maybe it is happiness for everyone who asks.
Maybe it is for what it is and never will be more.

Does it matter?

∞

ENGLISH
1998

Hey you, I am still talking!
I am freezing. It is cold outside.
Am I inside as I know there is warmth?
For I know the cold the coldness surrounds me.
Let me be the core as the core might cure me.
Am I walking ´purely´ for the fun of it?
Is purity what is left as the core appears on top?
May the core be the stone
thrown in the ocean to be on ground.
Is the ground overlaying the ´core´
or does the core not see the light because of the depth?
Does the stone open the world to its brightness
as love may overcome death of life?
May the bird pick up the stone
as the fish brings it up to the climaxing unsteady layer.
May the bird fly to the garden
as the core can cure at the nourishing place.
May the stone purify as the core
which will grow to a plant that overcomes.
Does it purify as I lie and let it fly towards the might?
And then where will it be again?
The stone that rolls down the mountain
and bounces off the ground for it might sink down the ocean.

Is it the same or just the similarity
which overwhelms you?

∞

Are you still listening?
Do you understand my written words
as they only subtly tell
my truth?

Felicity

Is it what you want when you dream at night?
Is it the wake up call destroying or enhancing?
Is it the end of the day that gives or takes hope?

Let it be the fantasy that comes to life.
Let it be the life that makes sense.
Let it be the sense that purifies the purpose.
Of all the meaning life has it takes so little.
Of all survivors bliss took of them so much.
Of all the talking they tell so little.
Villains may always be there.

Virtuosity shall always be there.
Very likely your own fate will let you choose your path.
Ending always as the strong?
Ending always as the faithful?
Ending always as the right one?

As for what it says tell me.
As for what I live let me.
As for what you want you shall.

∞

Again, gorgeous, again.
Do you not regret not listening to me?
As for compromising matters
I do not agree with you.
As for politics come to life
I do not see you.
Does becoming a politician
give you the tender moments
you need for bliss in life.
Do you really care when you argue
or is it just that you want to be
on spot?
Do you draw the line or do you recommend privacy
only for the pious?

Exhilaration overcomes you.
Is it for the one or for the many?
Do you second your fear
of being let alone with your dreams
as images appear showing life as life could be
diverging with reality that yours is,
being painfully reminded of what you do not have
and might never have – it is your life.
Are you popular? Do you feel popular?
Or do they just think of you as popular?!
May they be them or thee
as life may be thy for them.
Am I obnoxious when I tell stories
you have neither planned nor opted for
or do I just try to level ground for you to stand on?

Just give your hand for me to hold
as I will guide you through the jungle.
Just use your feet to step on me
as I will walk you through the flames.
Just take the seat I have prepared
as I will drive you through the desert
to an oasis occurring as obvious.

Let me pierce you for I will show you
the blue flame as blue may not be the only color.
Let me let you lay down for I will lead you
to the garden as where leaves will smile by your encounter.
Let me read to you for the tales may reach the real
as imagination may fly towards the sky which will show its mercy.

Surrounded by the light you will not show
for you will not bore the stainless with your soul.
Sequenced by the questions you will laugh at them
for you will know that dreams brought life back to you.
Sentenced to life for life may be the life as life was meant to be.
...Points...
Enlighten the darkness with secrets of your own
as they being told may open doors not yet revealed.
End the turmoil, be succinct towards the ones
who want to get the keys which open the world.
Enrich the ones with joy for only you are capable to
as the ones are defined to be the ones who may receive.
...Points...

Jokingly
overwhelming
you.

∞

Father's Day

Tradition comes along.
Its meaning not always
truly appreciated.

´What for?´ our fathers said.
The deed had not been hard
contrasting the consequences
that followed along.
´Too hard to bear?´ you ask
and they laugh at you
not considering the *past*,
living in the *present*
and smiling at the *future*.

Asking yourself:
´What have I accomplished?´
´What have I received?´
´What have I forgotten?´

´Have I sought the right way?´
´Have I seen the signs?´
´Have I juxtaposed the priorities
towards the outstanding picture
I was capable of taking?´

you conclude:
Precious as life may be.
It was, is and will be
always worth it.

May worries be the past.
May happiness be the present.
May appreciation be the future.

Cents for life

∞

Time passing by.
Does it ever stop?
Can we still feel ourselves?

Formatting anything without objective purpose.
Forgetting the meaning of being.
Fencing the question of circulating the essential.
Oppress your will – we will hear.
Or may we choose – do you care?
Offering the simple – does it work?
Remind me – I am responsible.
Rest in duty – chant the required.
Rules engaged – no victory reached.

Which of you will volunteer?
Whenever needed – anybody.
Wrestling the Why – you do not ask.
While you follow you do not think.
Hey, good for you.
Heap me with orders.
Henceforth I will function.
Hereupon I will close my chapter.
Ask me not – I will not tell.
Acquaint yourself with ignorance.
Adhere yourself to the normal way.
And I guarantee it will stay simple.
Tutor your feelings – nobody cares anyway.
Truth has its beauty.
Tentative movements – as if it mattered.
Trust – there is nothing more precious.

???

Tales will never be told
as nobody cares.

∞

Hi, gorgeous. I have waited.
Do you recall what I asked you to?
You told me to open my soul.
I begged, cried, and, eager to please,
finally did it.
As I recovered I wished
everything undone
for there was no difference
I could feel.
You stood there laughing,
asking me what I had expected,
what I had been thriving for.
Hardly capable of speech I uttered:
„I love you!"
You said: „Someday, when you
look up and the sky is of clear blue
you will know where to find me."
Then you were gone.

And I stood there lying.
After rendering myself to the edge.
Although remembering the intrinsic of hers.
Letters to be written yet missing.
Lightness to its swiftness in remains.
Labor to lavish the lust in reserve.
Lacking the elements of complexion.
Limiting the thoughts to the bearable.
Levitate between loan and load.

Lessen the restrictions in sight.
Lessen the burden which breaks me.
Lessen the distance since the need becomes greater.
In doubt I am concerning your attitude.
Indeed I yearn after yours or maybe it is a mere illusion.
In fact I urge you to appear for insecurity of mine.

Expand my mind for it narrows during the daily.
Extract your pictures in the name of your inner secrets.
Enlarge yourself so the broad angle can be floated.
Surmise my most intimate wishes.
Surprise me with the unexpected, please.
Secure the links to our island.

74

Here I am,
little boy walking up the size.
Is little large or maybe honest?
After reprimanding myself for the questions
I lie down on the sand and look up.
I am bewildered,
cannot cope with what I see.
It is just unbelievable.
There it is
the clear blue sky.
I am finally capable of perceiving
the entire picture.
After an endless search
I ultimately found you,
my elusive gorgeous.

But,
what is there?
What fallacious sight?
Is it blue or just gray?

Where are you?

∞

As it was it never can.
Words nugatory for only
an impertinent reason.

Great men forgotten – who cares?
Gossip foresworn lasting lifetimes.
General morale pronounced – changing too often.
Irrelevance being the essence of life.
Imprudent calls – as lust is led to open.
Incarnate evil – the daily sight.
Vengeance is mine or maybe not.
Very much the need – the lesser the cause.
Vibrant as the corner appears – disillusion.
Energizer not given for let us part life.
Endless winter – white magic?
Everyone takes as no one does.

Mild wind traveling – do you follow?
Mild rain dropping – do you listen?
Mild, mild, mild – hard?
Elsewhere – only – does it happen?
Elsewhere – only – does fate lead to hope?
Elsewhere – only – does someone live?

And who said we did not choose?
And why said who we did?
And how said who why we chose?
Not for you, not for me, not even for us.
Neither this one nor the other one of the two doors.
Never pushed yet pulled this way.

Ask a dog for its ears.
Ask a cat for its eyes.
Ask a bird for its wings.
Night–flights as wings can take you.
Night–sights as far as eyes comply.
Night–sounds as ears can catch.
Sensing the world's needs like the creatures.
Seducing the world by shining bright.
Securing the world's failure by thoughts.
Wishes gaily sent – received unmentioned.
Whipped as righteous – demean with care.
Wills exclusively spoken – evaporate unheard.
Even you have been recognized before.
Elaborate the line untouched of grief.
Evince the bliss foregone and closed.
Relieve the part full of scorn.
Relinquish the mind set on revenge.
Rest the ones who let it linger.

Please – ask not why.
Please – dare not to look.
Please – no incentive, trust me.

Out of words, out of breath, out of touch.
In my way, in my hands, in my sight.

I, myself, to you, within yourself.

For the cause!
Which one?
Any way.

∞

White virgin

Did I ever mention I dream of you?
Since you have opened my eyes
my life cannot be the same.

At top or bottom – you vanquish.
Magnificent greatness of endless strength
easily enduring the roughness of climate
lasting forever
with infinite wisdom.

Seeing you from far away
makes shivers of bliss run through me
as I may be allowed to observe you.

Every crystal that visits you
is part of the dress that perfects
your beauty.

When I stand at your bottom and touch your skin
– hard and cold – I believe I can feel you.
In hope that you will accept me
I try you.
Filled with fear and respect
I move upon you
reaching for my goal
to be on top of you.

You let me and I achieve.
Words cannot describe how I feel.
Depicting my dreams,
your climax is my climax.

Please let me again.

∞

It will take time.
Patience – so I was told.

Negligence of bearing.

Imbibe yourself with thoughts.
Redeem your conscience.

Asking yourself while waiting
not if you have the time
but if you have the will
to endure.

Maybe you reckon on beliefs,
on society or none of both.

Seizing subtle insults plainly apparent
you are forced to acknowledge that
sometimes dreams may be made of vapor.

Only then do we feel
yet differing chances.

We would live
as if we had not been told
– just, just lived.

Is justly just just just when prone
to opinionated society?

Do we suffer or do we gain
by thinking the thoughts yet unthought but to be openly thought?

Capability of whom – thy?
Reasoning, what for – thee?
Caressing the tried reply, why – thy?

Carefree environmental digest.
Celestial practical surplus.
Cumulating evidential malfunction.
Respective fostering blossom.
Rendering incessant pursuit.
Reiterating local process.
Continental fueling decrease.
Cultural disobedient requisites.
Cure coy vacancy.

Cosmic reality consumes.

Outmatched by the burden of avocation
or the need to wait until it has arrived.

Can you believe just that?

As time will tell
shall we use principles of the past?

Creativity
paired with imagination.
Imagination
paired with fantasy.

Character
paired with personality.
Personality
paired with honor.

Negligible obligations to be omitted?

Are you able
to swallow the load
or do you
suffocate while trying?

∞

ENGLISH
1999

Light changes.
Terrific moments fleeing its origin.
What gives?
What in hell does make the take away?
Compelled by its beauty.

Telling – help me, does it?
Tremble – if not it may.
Trust employs – voyage incomplete.
Reference in demand – change its attitude.
Resemblance on its own – fear me.
Rusty parts – winter does not apply.
Undertake measures unforeseen – beauty calls.
Undress its bottom – let the top take away.
Undermine the motive – forgive me if it does.
Sure you are – are you not that if you are?!
Survive the top – tearing off the bottom?
Syllables addressed – in itself if itself inside.
Tense if you may – windows may open.
Transcend the plant – just wish.
Turbulence awaiting – never mind its cause.

Only now do you have the picture in red.
Will if you may – appalled by its beauty.
Do you mind setting yourself towards it?
Do you really – if not, then never to be.

Let me tell you.
Do you wish to?
Then it shall be.

Remember flowers blossoming.
Just as it becomes apparent.
Remember walking through jungles.
Unforeseen to where the path leads.
I told you about the mountain.
It comes to my mind knocking down the plant.
Just why?

Just because it is – greater.
Just because may not be the reason
nor be sufficient.
Is it still enough for the call?!

Beauty rings – just where does it lead to?
It may hurt badly – do you really want it?
Surged in its sense – it will finally strike!
No concerns whatever of the top.
Relinquished to the bottom.
Forgetting the roots – human mankind is likely to.
Is hurting equal to healing?
One might think so.
You ask me if I do?
I do.

Too many of them said
– forever –
nourishing only their own,
not thinking about consequences
nor hardly about the blossoming flower.

Do you receive power by destroying
or by challenging the obstacles?
One might think so.
Do I?
No, I do not.

At last is what at least a lot of them said.
Forgiving is an option.
One might think so.
Do I?
Cannot answer.

Believe or not – I have seen the blossoming
take place.
Does it hurt?
Yes, it does – very much.
Do I believe?
Yes, I do.
Yes, I do believe, remembering
the gorgeous one.
How come?

Well, once upon a time
a prince was called to call in progress.
He did not fall for whichever
trap was laid.
He just believed
connecting
beauty in itself, forever.

Then, eternity took place.
Being die hard he finally came to a solution.
Only beauty connected with its eternity
was to be gorgeous.

At least he believed,
albeit consciousness could have been capable
of overtaking him.
Still he believed.
Not in its original sense, not in any known variables
but still he was sure what for!

Despite the pain that would prelude
he knew every stone crushed
would be worth it –just to reach his aim:
to find the gorgeous one.

Relentless of the actions to be taken to achieve
he knew he had fought, was fighting and would be fighting
just to compensate his aim,
maybe for the cause,
maybe for himself
but surely for its beauty.

Realizing hell was close to heaven
he found a way to ambush his dreams.
While doing that he could not think further
as to which his dreams of the gorgeous led him.

Reckoning on his visions he thought it likely
to find a way
back to balance.
Calling back on the edges,
helpless of its obstructions to take place,
hopeful to resurrect the beach

to land on
he fought on and on and on,
only to find that it may be hopeless
to pursue in respect to opportunity.

Still he went on,
thinking only about the gorgeous,
since her beauty compelled him
to abiding other possible ways to proceed.

To be king in his own kingdom
was not that hard,
he knew.
But to find her beauty and her love
he assembled the facts that
being king might not increase his chances.

Going on as just a simple man
he was thrilled by the possible encounter
to finally reach the top
by not neglecting the bottom
and to receive the trust
enabling an encounter with her,
just her – the gorgeous.

Trembling by the thought
it was enough
to pursue his goal
to assume happiness
by achieving
his aim
to meet her – gorgeous.

Never giving up.

Wish you were here!

∞

What about the world, gorgeous?
Told him to move, did you?!
Break up with the truth, will you?!
Betrayal of life awaits you
if you do not, does it?

I just read about you.
Made me smile, you know.
Self–conscious as I may be
still I know what good
I can do.
Can I?
Who knows
but you
if you were to entangle.

As bright as the colors maybe
there still is something amiss.
Do you trust my judgement?
I guess not, albeit
I know you would if you came
to meet me on stable grounds.
All I always wished for – you in person.
Do I really think so?
Not sure anymore.

What if the truth embedded within society
cannot be counted for as the overall truth
I have been seeking for so far?
Have you been giving thoughts to the overall picture
or just lived up to the reality given?
One might think so
as I may do, do I?
Sensing?!
I come to think that it was hopeless
from the very beginning to even let
yourself fool into that illusion.
I wonder why you did not
flash a sign ahead of time.
Did you like me in the dark?

Oh, you wanted to get ready
before you receive me.
How nice of you.
Three eternities of waste.
Three consecutive tear–downs that,
not considering the time passed before
– without knowing–
might have led to different styles.
Waste,
which at surely tedious surroundings
might be called preparation after all,
might have been worth it
considering the journey.
Do I really think so?
Compelled by the answer,
the answer is yes.
What is yours?
Oh, I forget,
you cannot answer.

Then just be ready
when the arrival in time has emerged.

I will be.

Fear
is final
and will not take over,
I am sure, not so sure.
Sure I am sure.
Damn right
I am sure.
I hope you will be,
if not,
perish at your destination.

I do not forget.
Never!

∞

Utmost it was
as it has always been.

Only now do we have
what will compromise
the need for steps.

Everyone there ever was
has always had their own ideas
bar any troubling messages.
Did you think so?
As I see the light in plain
I try to envision
the concave
in breaking the blue.

What does it take
to convince you
of the utmost need?

cut
dream
cut

Forever is hopeless I know
but now I will escape
and my evasion
will be successful.
How do I know?
I just do.

Come and look
into my eyes.
They will tell.
They will always tell.
Who cares but me
as I will go and do.
Did you see
the train pass by?

I did.

Did you smell
the sour odor?
I did not.

Did you recognize
the pulchritude?
I did.
I guess I was
not to fear her.
Was I not?
Should I not?
Maybe.

I am frightened
but please, please,
do not tell
anyone
who might advance.

What I cared for,
was I cured of?
Yes and no,
not even sure if I should.

Hey, you know,
it is really
that
you never thought so.
Did I?
Who cares?
Do I?
Never to tell.

Say hi.
Be free.
Never to make sense.

∞

Treasures untaken,
worlds apart,
left for good?

See through me.
Let mileage be.
On foot to transfer.
A wanderer to be joined.
As we leave we are to be.
Embrace the good.
It is to happen to us.
Bound to and well received.
I will be there also.

Light-hearted walking up the path.
I know there will be followers.

I will not dispense of them
but truly not let them threaten
the pace I walk my way.

I will do no matter what,
joined by the ones
who started walking by themselves.
I reckon it will be us.
Tracking others will not show.

Illuminate your path
– freedom may be new –
it will shine upon others
who will receive the light.

To have led
may have been the cause.

∞

To the last ones

Somebody told me I have been there.
Since somebody is not anybody,
I started to believe.
Maybe I should have stayed by myself.
To define myself I would have to go all the way.
Will do – certainly.
Future and past – comparison made.
What has been cannot be – can it?
Has the keeper lived forever?
Did the piano start playing?
Has the door been open before somebody went inside?
Was there somebody not afraid as the real one appeared?
As he stands there – drawing.
As the folks start noticing.
As real life begins to unveil.
As the cowards drop to the floor
they know they will be the first ones
to leave the stage.
You stand there and you know
it will spread as long as you stay.
Since cowboys never stay for long
you know the wanderer will be on his way
to check if unnecessary changes have been made.

Somebody will speak up – it has always been.
Courage non-withstanding – honor presides.
What of impertinences that you flouted.
As being there might help solving.
If I see you I know a few things beforehand.

He is the one who is going to walk his way.
He is the decision-maker up front.
He shall overcome if nothing else.
He will invent unforeseen interchangeables.
He leads – following not open to option.
He will find a path uncovered yet.
The search might go on forever.
While at it, he has already seen the light.
The code reminds as followed.

You shall be given honor.
You shall honor your privileges.
Your privileges shall be your capacity.
Your capacity shall always remain.
Your remains shall always incinerate.
Your incineration shall lead the faithful.
Your faith shall be full of pride.
Your pride shall be forever.
– As forever pride is unforgotten –
You shall forever be in light.
Your light shall be your resource.
Your resource shall never struggle.
Your struggle shall always concentrate on yourself.

You will always be the one
who will lead the way,
who will initiate changes,
who will always be on top,
who will show the example,
who will point to different directions,
who will always be the one
and nothing else.
There is nothing else to be.
Since we live we are.

Up front and never showing,
deep inside the core is knowing.
Since the body reacts
we know
what we do
in any case.

We lived.
We live.
We will live.
In any case.

∞

Transcend upon me like heaven.

Fulfil options yet unconcern'd.

As to you it is with raven;

Cease me for you I yearn´d.

As dark in silver was her mood,

And feather's wit was there to shine.

Its finding less than might its root.

For every bit driven not yet mine.

May I be free as free is able.

May I see the world like you.

As matters far end is favorable,

Deem the sky as clear and blue.

Just when you had and will not give,

Just then it is that I may live.

∞